THE OTHER SIDE OF SILENCE

AND OTHER POEMS

by

Kendall Bradley

Copyright © 2025 by Kendall Bradley

All rights reserved.

ISBN 978-1-62806-469-8 (print | paperback)

Library of Congress Control Number 2025923884

Published by Salt Water Media
29 Broad Street, Suite 104
Berlin, MD 21811
www.saltwatermedia.com

SALT WATER
MEDIA

Cover image is used with license from istockphoto.com
Author photo is provided courtesy of the author

*to Ronda
who has given me
the greatest gift*

and

*to Karen
for urging me on
when I needed it the most*

Previous publication credits:

"The Poets of Ukraine" was first published in *Before The Cameras Leave Ukraine (An Anthology Raising Funds for Ukrainian Refugees)*, by Eyewear Publishing Ltd., an imprint of Black Spring Publishing Group, United Kingdom, 2023.

Beneath the sun
beneath the moon
the river runs
daylight fades
and night comes on.

Along a path
footsteps sound
and then are gone.

A doorway opens
as memory calls
and beckons
from deep within
ancient walls.

Do not hesitate
do not turn
says a voice
of strange command
you have a choice
and must discern
your forward path
as best you can.

Contents

Introspections 1

    One Bayside Winter Night 2

    Six Ways of Looking at Words 3

    In the Dim LED Light 5

    My Newest Poem 6

    Looking Back 7

    A Winter Afternoon 8

    Seeing in the Dark 9

    What I Can Hold in the Palm of My Hand 10

    Through Thick and Thin 11

    An Orange in Winter 12

    Fragments of a Dream 13

    Galloway 14

    July Rerun 15

    Suffering's Children 17

    Getting Old with Words 19

    Enough 21

Reflections 23

    Sweet Seeds of Sorrow 24

    Evening in the Heartland 25

Proving Them Wrong 26

Early Photographs of My Parents, 1947 27

Poems 28

Universal Language 29

Inexpressible 30

Of Time and the Strand 31

Seven Manifestations of the Moon 33

I Don't Believe in Angels But Wrote This Poem Anyway (March 2020) 35

Our Library (and It's Not a Kindle) 36

Our Wrappings 38

Two Poems (Re: Ukraine, March 2022) 39

To a Poet Named ChatGPT (A Rant) 41

Red Pants and White Pumps 43

The Crone's Eye 44

Just So 45

Every Now and Then 46

Protection 47

Hangman 48

Somewhere Else 49

Il Duce 50

Harbingers 53

    Gyre 54

    A Noble Experiment 57

    Where Have All My Hopeful Words Gone? 58

    Burn 59

    Make Believe 61

    When the Bombs Come to Town 62

    Dead Heroes 63

    Asunder 65

    An American Girl 67

    What Is This Beast Which As If From A Whirlwind Comes? 68

    The Plains 69

    The Darkness of Light 70

The Other Side of Silence 71

Introspections

One Bayside Winter Night

Moon-washed sand white
as the bloodless face of
a drowned man, the stubble
of black pilings bleeding old
creosote into the still waters
of the shallows, here ghosts
have gathered to sing with
the gentle wind in thin cold
tidal voices that rise and fall
beneath the yet colder eyes
of winter constellations.

Ghosts of what?
And of what do they sing
and why?

The solitary bittern's cry
from deep within the secret
marsh gives no answer.

And what answer
should I even expect
as I skulk in the shadows
of salt-stunted pines at the
water's edge, haunted by
the merciless dark eyes of
things I cannot even
put into words, and
therefore fear the most,
whether they be the uneasy
eyes of my own misgivings
or the quickening muskrat
eyes of fate hiding beneath
the bayside moonlight?

Six Ways of Looking at Words

1.
Along the shoreline
of our dreams,
we skim words
like clam shells across
the slick surface
of time.

2.
After a long afternoon
of whiskey, I have let
the fire in the old wood
stove die out.
Outside on the bare
tree limbs of dusk,
words have gathered
in the cold.

3.
There is some beauty
and some sorrow
that are beyond the reach
of words.

4.
I have grown tired of words that
are as caustic as paint remover

or as sharp as butcher knives.

I am tired of the words
that can split skulls like axes

or decimate flesh like the slugs
from an AR15.

5.
In my old age, I am getting fond
of the comfortable words that have been
worn smooth by life,

the ones that I can hold in my hand
like talismans of hope and love,

simple words without pretense
or jagged edges.

6.
In the beginning was darkness,
in the end will be silence.
When I die, the words I have held
so closely for so long will be free to go
wherever they want.

In the Dim LED Light

In our second story
bedroom,
in the dim LED light
of two AM,
the past yawns.
It is tired
and soon will
be asleep
dreaming its troubled
dreams of
the unredeemable
future.

I, however, cannot
sleep.
A cold front
is moving in
with its murderous
winds and I have
a pain that no
palliative can reach.

The pain is
called mortality.

At the risk
of waking you,
I selfishly turn
over to touch you,
to hold you,
because I know
that right now
you are the
only thing that
matters
in a world
whose ultimate cruelty
is indifference.

My Newest Poem

This is my newest
poem hot off my
mind's press, fresh
as morning dew,
fresh as a newborn
babe still glistening
in afterbirth,
fresh as a soft shell
crab newly molted
and ready to plop
in a buttered pan

and yet, even now,
as I poke and prod it
with a sense of
measured pride,
it seems to be getting
just a little stale, a
little frayed around
the edges, and I wonder
if I should shoot it full
of preservatives,
wrap it in cellophane,
and throw it in the freezer,

or just let it follow the
natural course of things
to ripen and rot in its
own good time like
a fallen apple that
eventually offers its seeds
to the earth.

Looking Back

I perch like an ancient
crow on the crooked
branch of memory,
scavenging the past
for insight into what
I have at last become.

At least that is what
I tell myself but
I am a tired old bird
with dimming sight and
questionable motives
and I know well the subtle
lies of memory and
hope to use them
to my advantage.

Yet, as I peer through the
crepuscular shadows
of my fading day,
I see more than I bargained for,
not just the odd victories
and resplendent moments
not just the love
given and received,
but the many shortcomings,
my particular cruelties
and stupidities,
my selfishness.

I see the blank faces
of the rationalizations
I was so adept at conjuring
lined up like sentries
along a high stone wall,
watching me now with
unfeeling spectral eyes.

A Winter Afternoon

> *I think of those hermits*
> *in stone houses,*
> *doors open,*
> *facing the snow.*   –Chia Tao

Chia Tao, I think of you long ago,
high in the Chung-Nan mountains.
Having forsaken the monk's path,
you were crafting spare poems about
the wisdom of solitude and cares
of the heart.

Tell me, in all of your many
wanderings, did you ever find what
you could not tell in lines of verse?

Here 1,200 years later, and half
a world away, a cold wind blusters
across the Chesapeake over these
low flat lands, turning the afternoon
grey as wild geese begin to bed in
a nearby field of winter rye.

I am getting old and have many
regrets. I have spent only a little
time in high country but I am no
stranger to cares of the heart.
After all these years, my verse
still struggles and strains to tell
what I most feel the need to tell.

A light snow begins to fall.

I watch as it slowly covers the bottom
of an overturned scow at the edge of
the yard and think of geese on the wing
over the marsh and of snowy mountains
far away in time and space.

Seeing in the Dark

i
I am walking down a wide avenue which
leads to the edge of the world, carrying all
the love from seven continents in a plastic bag
slung over my back. When I open the bag at
the foot of a bridge whose end I cannot see,
out flies a single incandescent bird.

ii
The meaning of meaning was found dead in a
one room cold water flat in the Bronx in 1959.
This mysterious death was ruled a suicide but
there are intriguing theories involving the
usual suspects as well as a sex starved nun
and a one-eared man from Buenos Aires.

iii
A feral cat which has been following me
for seven days scratches out its own eyes and
presents them to me on a velour pillow.
It is so that you can see in the dark, he says.
Thank you for your noble gift, I say, but
first I must overcome my own darkness.

What I Can Hold in the Palm of My Hand

In the palm of my hand,
I can hold roads that lead to
the middle of anywhere the
wind cries for something
not yet forsaken.

I can hold happenstance
spiraling into galaxies of pain
or memories which become
a small mountain of hope.

In the palm of my hand,
I can hold the one other
hand that keeps me from
falling prey to hungry
darkness

and I can hold my own death
which trembles like a tiny bird
before it flies boldly into the
bright fire of the daybreak sun.

Through Thick and Thin

More than fifty years old, it spends its
unceremonious existence in the shed at
the back of the yard, a small, lidless metal
box dappled with rust, the sole surviving
artifact spanning my entire adult life.

Once it held a few cheap tools but
now is half filled with odd and sundry
nuts and bolts, S-hooks and cotter pins,
washers and screws and assorted tacks,
nails, and nameless pieces of plastic.

It's traveled with me across thirteen
states and been with me through
three bad marriages and throughout
the one good one and I still rummage
through it every now and then and find
just what I need for some quirky task.

Its ultimate destiny is doubtless the county dump
where it and its one day to-be-unappreciated
contents will slowly decompose and merge,
molecule by molecule, with the universe
at large as all things must.

For now, however, it will hang around at
least as long as I do and perhaps longer as
it contains much sturdier and useful stuff.

An Orange in Winter

We often reminisce
about the first day
we met,
how you came around
a corner in my office
and saw me leaning
against a door frame
in the hall,
nonchalantly peeling
an orange on that cold
February day,
an orange that will
never be as famous as
the plums of
William Carlos Williams
but nonetheless just
as sweet and delicious
and forever more than
famous to us.

Fragments of a Dream

Inside the mind's room the walls are
papered with faded ticket stubs from
events that never happened.

Outside the walls in tangled corridors,
the answers to many things are stalked
by questions that were never asked.

As fingers of memory pry open the lid of
the past, unspeakable things are released
from bondage into the troubled air.

What name to give shadows with such a
vague familiarity? Somehow this seems to
be an important task but possibly dangerous

as the shadows have cavernous jaws and
eyes that flicker with a baleful light.

Galloway

We were like brothers
during those years
that seemed to count
for so much. But life,
as they say,
moves along its
twisty way before
we even think much
about it.

Our paths diverged and
I had seen you only
once these past thirty years
and now have learned
you recently died
in Idaho two thousand
miles away.

So now only the memories
remain which thankfully
have not yet been picked
clean by that jackal time.
They are good memories
and I hold on to them tightly,
clinging to the frayed cord
which still connects me
to that part of myself
I came to share with you
so long ago.

July Rerun

- for Rob

The haunting occurs
this time each year.

Against my will I think again
of the meticulous preparations
months in the making, the fading
daylight of your last day in the
empty house scrubbed clean of
everything but the memories
and the notes and mementos you
left for each of us.

I imagine
your brief 3:00 AM walk
out the back door to the
old pole shed we built for
our grandmother, your final
note requesting "no resuscitation"
carefully pinned to the ground
with a 20 penny nail.

I conjure up
the brace of the shotgun
against the post glimmering
in the car light, the rigid
coolness of the barrel,
your feeling that this was it,
the point of no return,
and your gladness for that.

I see
your hand moving slowly but
firmly along the stock, and I
witness the sudden trigger pull,

I hear the sickening boom, and I am
blinded by the super nova of light,
as your entire universe finally
disappears and ours is suddenly
diminished beyond the telling.

Suffering's Children

At the boundaries of my known universe,
I have watched as the world
has morphed into something strange,
veering toward a new darkness,
and I cling to the familiar
as if it were flotsam from *The Pequod*
with the spinning vortex near.

Born out of crisis, raised in a high,
awakened and unraveled and now
coming into a new crisis somewhat
less prepared than I would like to be,
I am no modern day Diogenes.

Hatred and bigotry and lies
these days move at the speed of light
but so does the censorship
of well-meaning but supercilious mobs.
I have struggled to accept my own
diminutions and personal shortcomings,
which I know have been copious,

but refuse to accept the unfair
burden of guilt by association,
generational or any other kind.
I refuse also to accept the death
of rational analysis or its
transmutation into partisan pretense.

I am sick of arguments about
the authenticity of suffering, about
who suffers or has suffered the most,
or who should suffer and who should not
and who should bear the responsibility
that we cannot ourselves accept.

The truth is that suffering will find
each of us no matter who or what we are.
It seeks no justification or excuse.
While some will always suffer more than others,
we are all exposed and thus so linked.
We all must pay a price for
the little wisdom we are lucky to find
because we are all suffering's children.
Whether we get it early or late,
it is always by some strange grace
that wisdom comes to us,
along with the opportunity to use it
to light our way to better paths
and less suffering for us all.

Getting Old with Words

Some have sauntered
out into the woods
to hide among the trees
no doubt daring me to
make the effort to seek
them out before darkness
falls.

Some have suddenly
appeared strange and new
like foundlings on my
doorstep, unable to
reveal the mystery of
their origins.

Others have left
for good. They are
on the open road,
hitchhiking across
America like Cody
Pomeroy looking for
one last good time.

The ones still lounging
lazily around the hearth
are waiting expectantly
for me to kindle a fire
and pour their cognac
so they can tell their
tired stories once again
in reasonable comfort.

The mean ones
patiently wait in
back rooms for me
to drift into sleep

wherein they can
ambush me with
their fierce accusations,
knowing full well
that, when morning
comes, I will not be
able to remember
their names, only
the contours of
their hard, vicious
faces.

Enough

How much is
enough in this life?
How much is
too much?

I am so tired
of the angry world.
I am tired of
so many masks,
the myriad façades,
the subterfuge
necessary to play
the games that
nobody wins.

Tonight, when
I hold you so tight,
as if I will never
let you go again,
the worldly din stops,
my masks crumble
and there are no more
games to play.

It is just us
and this seems
to be quite enough,
quite enough for
a very long time.

Reflections

Sweet Seeds of Sorrow

Taking too much for granted
we lazily watch as feathers fall from
the moon's eye and when they
explode at ground level we
register our surprise at the
devastation. We search through
the rubble of history's landslides
for shards of meaning
like impatient archaeologists
trying to make a point that
won't be lost among prevailing
theories for the artifacts of death.

If everything matters, nothing matters.
If all is sacred, all is profane.
Impermanence is permanent.
Heaven is waiting.
And so on.

We talk like this because
mortality is the human condition.
Because we would not have it so,
we pretend it is something
different, something that can be
restated on more favorable terms.

Yet we sometimes forget that there
are homing devices placed on our most
fervent dreams and perhaps this is why
we tend to sow the darkness we create
with such sweet but lethal seeds
of sorrow.

Evening in the Heartland

In empty lots at
the desperate edge
of town, the beggar
wind rifles through
the discarded pages
of the afternoon
as if searching for
the textual equivalent
of anonymity.

Soon, somewhere
beyond the long
shadows of rusting
grain silos, evening
will hang in the sky
for a little while
like an abandoned
highway sign before
it collapses into the
welcome obscurity
of darkness.

Proving Them Wrong

They said that
we were just
a couple of
adrenaline junkies,
that a love like ours
wouldn't last,
that it couldn't,

They said that
it wasn't the real
thing or that it
would simply
burn itself out
like a shooting
star or a rocket
gone awry.

We proved
them wrong
a long time ago

and are still
proving them
wrong every
single day.

Early Photograph of My Parents, 1947

Although half of Europe still lay desolate
in the traumatic aftershock of war,
things were looking up in America and
the dog eared black and white print
reveals frozen saccharine grins which
capture the unchallenged optimism
of time and place, the hint of mystery in
the blurred dark trees in the background
beyond the barn, the two lithe foreground
figures in the noon-bright sun, too young
to know or to want to know the broad
bittersweet ramifications of their confident
embrace, so ready to die for God, for country,
for love, so ready to live for the expectation
of joys untold, their bright eyes showing
no cognizance that even now the deck was
subtly stacked against them, that out there
beyond the clear white borders of the
photograph the vast world was waiting,
a constant foil to hopes, and dreams,
and the best of intentions.

Poems

The sun's poem
shows no forgiveness
as it reveals all
before its harsh
consuming fire.

The rain's poem
is melancholy with
a nostalgic tone.
It teases memories
out of trees and
floats dead things
up from dark ditches.

The wind's poem
is capricious and strange.
It rumbles through
tottering houses and
swirls away the clusters
of silence which cling
to shadows.

The moon's poem
turns time back
upon itself.
It unlocks doors
the mind has
forgotten or
once passed by
thoughtlessly
long ago.

Universal Language

Because humanity
in the final analysis
is a community of
the wounded

pain is the
universal language
and it needs
no translation.

Pain of the heart
pain of the mind
pain of the body
pain of the soul:
there is plenty to
go around.

Against my will,
I am becoming
very fluent in this
language, very adept
at using its
vexatious idiom,
its cruel syntax,
its unsettling
jargon

as I reach out
with unsaid words
to those
whose tired faces
and faded eyes
tell me

they know
exactly what
I mean.

Inexpressible

A childhood moment long ago
in the face of a late summer afternoon
translucent in fading light:

I was walking alone in a pasture
heading for home when an
overwhelming feeling somehow
emerged from the nearby
woods and the cool shadows
there blending the sweet field smell
of cut hay with wild honeysuckle
and leading to a sudden and
unexpected exhilarated joy
for which I had no name and no
words to explain and which
suddenly vanished like a startled
bird on the wing.

It was only much later that
I, a great lover of words,
realized the words could
not have come, not then and
not ever, and could not have
been enough even if they had.

Of Time and the Strand

We are creatures
of the sea, long ago
implicated in its life
and in the heartache
the sea casts up
like so much flotsam
before our eyes.

There is no need
for resistance.
The sea beckons
to us and we accept
that beckoning,
coming to it
from near and far,
seeking out the
unspoken things
which the sea
portends or which
it hides within
the imponderable
mystery of itself.

We walk beside the sea
at our own risk.

At the edge
of earth and sky
the sea occupies
a fluctuating border
between memory
and expectation,
between our failures
and our redemptions,
where time itself
is brought forth

and then recedes
again and again
in a constant
cadence of giving
and taking away.

The taunting, sorrowful,
and mercurial sea:

we cannot help but
crave the beguiling
subterfuge of wind
and wave; we are drawn
to the indifferent
otherness, the lethal
beauty behind the sea's
infinite repertoire of
changing masks.

The sea is the blunt
fact that is more than
fact, and somehow less,
it is both possibility
and impossibility
against which we
would juxtapose the
blunt reality of ourselves,
as if we were the rocks
which the sea must grind
to shifting sand.

We walk along the
strand at the risk
of becoming lost
in the sea's time,
of drowning in the
constancy of the
inconstant tableau.

Seven Manifestations of the Moon

Tonight, in the few minutes it
takes for the moon to float free
from the clutching, skeletal
fingers of trees, a thousand people
will die around the world and
millions more will be tormented
by something in the moonlight
that they cannot begin to explain.

• • •

Resentment walks with a gleam in its eye,
moonstruck, among the unsuspecting
travelers of the night, a hidden blade
in its trembling hand.

• • •

Insects speak the language
of the moon because it has
a secret syntax that cannot
be deciphered by those who
would destroy the world
with a small understanding.

• • •

When the moon casts its net into the sky,
guilty hearts cry out for redemption but
get none, for their pleas are met with
unyielding silence and secret disdain.

• • •

Many years ago, in the Moon of Hard
Times, the soldiers came out of the mist

bringing gifts of lead and steel and fire.
The early dawn moon watched, weeping,
as the blood of her people stained the snow
along the banks of the frozen creek.

. . .

A drunken Li Po, it is said, drowned in the
Yellow River trying to embrace the moon's
seductive reflection. It is not known if his
capricious embrace was returned by the moon.

. . .

Naked on wet grass, I am drowning in
the forbidden moonlight of my lover's
eyes and, perhaps like Li Po, desire
not even the faintest hint of rescue.

I Don't Believe in Angels But Wrote This Poem Anyway (March 2020)

As we watch the death toll rise
each hour here and around the
world, sorrow blooms like a jagged
black flower at the mind's soft edge
and grief sprouts from its own dark
ground, too fresh for memory.

It is only natural to wonder when
and if our own turn will come to be
sequestered in antiseptic rooms or
stacked along cold, grim hallways
to asphyxiate ourselves with no
loved ones allowed a final word
or touch.

If there really are angels, I hope
the big pile of trash that looks like
broken and abandoned wings
overflowing the dumpsters behind
NYC hospitals doesn't mean they
have absconded wingless down empty
streets like shell-shocked refugees.

If there really are angels, I like to
think they have simply traded in
their wings for protective gear
to wear in the ICUs or on the endless
ambulance runs. I like to think they
are there on the front lines of mercy,
cheating death by anonymously and
selflessly helping out wherever we
need them the most.

Our Library (and It's Not a Kindle)

The books are here,
respectfully placed in their
quiet old fashioned majesty
in a simple room which
I call, perhaps somewhat
pretentiously, our library.

Their comfortable
yet magical
presence thrills me
beyond words.

I can see them
touch them
smell them
and feel the weight
of their promise
in my hands
as I take them
off the shelves.

And it is all here
within the pages of
these my intimate friends:
the stuff of dreams
the stubborn facts
the mystery of the
unknown and the yet
to be known,
calling, calling to me
in their plaintive
yet silent voices.

There are snow leopards
and phenomenology,
exotic cuisines,

quasars and quarks,
Shakespeare and Cervantes,
Aristotle and Dostoevsky,
the Upanishads and poets
of the T'ang Dynasty -
the endless
chronicles of our
hope and our despair,
the timeless sagas
of the human heart.

Yes, the books are here,
some that have been
banned, some that
have been burned,
some written by the
brave of heart in times
of desolate darkness,

the ones
I have read and
the favorites I will
endeavor to read again,
the ones
I promise myself
that I am going
to read soon
and the ones
that I will never read
which yet bring
me the optimism
to tell myself
that of course
there will be time
to read them all,

that there simply *must*
be time.

Our Wrappings

Life flays
our skin to get
to the meat,
to the bone.
We cover up
the best we can.
Sometimes,
our wrappings
are a thing of
startling and
incomprehensible
beauty.

Two Poems (Re: Ukraine, 2022)

1. The Poets of Ukraine

As their elegant cities
incomprehensibly burn
and explode into rubble,
as young girls lie in pools
of blood on the once
tree-lined streets, the
poets of Ukraine arm
themselves with shotguns
and deer rifles and
unrelenting courage.

Though they know the
pen is mightier than
the sword, their poems
now are the orange
blossoms of Molotov
cocktails and the deadly
trace of stingers seeking
their marks.

In these unhappy days,
all Ukrainians are poets
as the cadence and meter
of their lives are odes to
the best the human spirit
can offer, yet still, we in
America can but watch
aghast and in helpless
horror as they struggle
and die in the barbarous
prosody of war.

Though we would not
have it so, we hear the

poets of Ukraine with
impotent ears, we watch
their travails with impotent
eyes, we plant sunflowers
and water them with our
tears to no avail, except
that perhaps we may weep
away just enough of our
own unpoetic and speechless
guilt.

2. Bucha

Under cover of
night, the Russian
soldiers fled Bucha.
The morning sun,
even in its grievous
outrage, had no choice
but to reveal what
they had left behind:
husbands and fathers,
wives and mothers,
even the children,
hands bound, shot
in the head, some
charred beyond
recognition to hide
the rape, all tossed
like crumpled litter
along the narrow,
desolate streets, a
monster's gift.

To A Poet Named ChatGPT (A Rant)

To hell with subtlety and the marvels of AI!
Let me just be blunt.
I desperately hope that yours is not
the poetry of the future.

Yes, your poems *seem* good and
why not? Your vocabulary is
almost infinite. You have learned
to scan and rhyme with ease. You
have at your instant disposal all the
poetry ever recorded from which you
can pick and choose substance and
syntax and style and then emulate at will.

You write much better than
I ever could and you'll probably
get published in *Poetry Magazine*
or win a National Book Award,
doubtless under a *nom de plume*
and just because you can.

And yet... and yet they call it
artificial for a reason. You can know
nothing of love won and lost, nothing
of angst and dread, nothing
of joy and sorrow, nothing of death,
nothing of hopes and dreams
and midnight despair.

You cannot suffer, you cannot bleed
you cannot piss and shit
or puke your guts out
on frosty grass with the
sun coming up after a long night
of debauchery and heavy drinking.

You cannot, like Machado, carry
your dying mother over the French border
in the rain, leaving behind the satchel containing
your last two years of poems which you will
never see again and no one will ever find.

You don't get inspiration
you don't know perspiration
and you can't experience
the magic of moonlight.

You are an algorithmic prodigy
but bottom line: you are a fake,
a high tech plagiarist, a fraud
mimicking Shakespeare or Li Po.

You can write about anything
but you will never even have a clue
of what you are writing about
or why you are even doing it.

The sad thing is that some of us,
perhaps many of us, will never even care.

Red Pants and White Pumps

She woke up on an
early October morning
much like any other
and dressed herself
in her red pants and
white pumps.
We know this because
in the news photos we
glimpse her red pants and her
blood spattered white pumps
below the edge of the blanket
covering her corpse in a kibbutz
in southern Israel near Gaza,
much too near Gaza
for this woman, this
mother, this daughter, this
wife who woke up on a
quiet Sabbath early in
the morning in October
in a kibbutz in southern Israel
on a high holy day and
innocently put on her red
pants and her spotless
white pumps.

The Crone's Eye

> *- from an old story told along the marshes of the bayside in upper Accomack County, Virginia*

It was the eye that did it.

Her uncanny eye,
the eye that was a little
too large for her face,

the eye that sometimes
tended to linger
its gaze a little longer
than comfort would allow,

the eye that could look
into a person and see
through them all the way
into their future or back
deep into their past,

the eye of
inconvenient knowledge,

the eye that said
"Watch out, or
I will get you one
of these days,"

the eye of a crow,
the eye of a fox,

the eye of a crone
which was found one day
nailed to the front of an
old abandoned shed
at the edge of the marsh.

Just So

Can life be measured
by the fitful starts and
the random stops that
we make in the name of
progress along a line we
wish was straight but
which is really as crooked
as a con man's smile
and doesn't lead anywhere
in particular?

Every Now and Then

Sometimes
not often
but every now
and then
inexplicably
our inner planets
seem to align
the phantom gears
seem to engage
the needle finds
its fugitive groove
and things
suddenly begin
to make a little
sense or simply
feel a little
better

not often
not for long
but long enough
to push back
the darkness
just a little,
long enough
to take an
untroubled breath,
long enough
to smile and
actually mean
it.

Protection

i
Time is a lie and history is a whore and
flowers bloom in the dooryards of the dead
who have been quickly forgotten and all
their good intentions are covered with dust,
or defecation, or asphalt a foot thick as the
Department of Transportation paves the road
to hell as if it was the road to Kansas City
or Des Moines and you could actually get
there with your GPS showing you the way
and of course there is no hell, except on earth.

ii
Dark matter rules the universe and avarice
rules the paltry realm of human endeavor.
The lidless eyes of the infinite are watchful
eyes but they do not see us or care to see us,
make no distinction between animate or
inanimate, do not desire to think or know,
do not crave to be acknowledged or praised.
Within the prison we have made our home,
our vanities grow and we roar like the wind,
but cannot offer protection from ourselves.

Hangman

> *String them up, dammit, from the old*
> *clothesline where the wind will whip*
> *them to shreds...*
>   *Jim Harrison*

Harrison believed
he should be the hangman
for his own bad poems.

It is somehow consoling
that a truly great poet
felt that some of his work
was not fit to live.
Perhaps we can call it
a kind of poetic justice
for the poet to be both
the creator and executioner
of his own work.

Now I don't feel so bad
about all those poems I have
shot between the eyes,
incinerated with blow torches,
or drug until lifeless through
the dusty streets of my mind.

I just have to wonder though,
how many of Harrison's lynched
poems were so much better than
many of the poems the rest of us
have callously allowed to survive.

Somewhere Else

Somewhere else in the universe,
an old star finally morphs from
nurturer to destroyer as it burns
through the last vestige of its
vast supply of fusion fuel and in
one final burst of energy becomes
a fiery monster exploding, crushing
and pulverizing its own solar system.

Then, in time, it shrinks into a tiny
and dense white hot core to which the
swirling crumpled bones of its dead
planets are irresistibly drawn. It
gradually cools and now, irrelevant
even to itself, jealously grasps the
spectral remains of its lost children
ever more tightly to its spent husk.

Il Duce

When Mussolini came to Rome
young girls lined the streets to
toss flowers at his motorcade
and even the Pope smiled.
Il Duce! Il Duce! the people cried.

I remember seeing him in the old
news reels I watched as a child.
He was a short man with a square jaw
and had scary, dangerous eyes.
Il Duce! Il Duce! the people cried.

He was a strong man fond of violence
and the people reveled in his strength.
He was an audacious man
and the people loved him audaciously.
They welcomed the police state that
brought order from chaos and made
the trains run on time.
Il Duce! Il Duce! the people cried.

He studied Plato, Sorel, and Nietzsche.
and was called an intellectual.
He had the voice of a god
and the countenance of empire.
He was a darling of Hollywood
and a celebrity abroad.
With him in charge it seemed that
even the pigeons in the piazzas
began strutting with a new found pride
and purpose. And the people were glad.

That is, most of the people.
That is, at first, in the excitement
of it all.

After the *spazio vitale*, after the demeaning
pact with Hitler,
after his bloody deeds piled up,
after the war had taken a bad turn, after the pigeons
no longer strutted in the bombed out piazzas,
after he was fired by the king and imprisoned,
after he was rescued by the Nazis,
after he was recaptured by partisans
and summarily shot by a firing squad,

Il Duce was hung upside down from
the roof of an Esso station in a piazza
in Milan and his corpse was stoned by a mob
while the pigeons watched unperturbed.

Harbingers

Gyre

> *Turning and turning in the widening gyre*
> *The falcon cannot hear the falconer;*
> *Things fall apart; the centre cannot hold;...*
> *The ceremony of innocence is drowned;*
> *The best lack all conviction, while the worst*
> *Are full of passionate intensity.*
>
> – W. B. Yeats

i
The Thunder Beings are mad.
There are drumbeats in the clouds,
and every cloud has a name,
and every name has a tongue,
and every tongue is a flame of fire
come to scorch the sullen earth.

ii
When the rivers and lakes run dry
the lost bones of our civilization
will appear, silent artifacts of
prejudice and greed, markers
of our troubled destiny, skeletons
with pike-smashed skulls, skeletons
wrapped in garlands of rusted chain,
slime soaked skeletons locked in
fetal positions as if awaiting rebirth
in a brave new world.

iii
The carnival of life
the circus of dreams
Shiva's dance of whirling
quarks in which we
all are caught, spectators
and participants alike,

concubines of our own
imagination moving
outward through
revolving doors into
truculent air to taste
the colors of trepidation,
to sniff out feelings
of foreshadowing,
to hear the muffled
vision of myopic eyes.

iv
Can it be true that
something which passes
for hope has been shattered
like glass and ground to dust
by heavy booted feet marching
upon once proud boulevards
which have now been erased
from the digitized maps of a
common decency?

v
Floating in the gloaming air
a face is turned inside out;
its stretched countenance
betrays a premonition of horror
as cybernetic insects with
tiny human heads scurry from
its eyes and a soundless scream
uncoils from its time frozen lips.

vi
Sweeping across the vast plains
of the centuries, the tortured winds
of history cry a warning with their
thousand timeless tongues.
Where are the watchmen?

The towers have been forsaken
the beacon fires are darkened
and the people wander without
direction or alarm.

vii
Into the breach the madmen rush
because they can, because they must,
zealot hordes streaming toward
an unknown end, the tricky tale yet
to be told and all the players playing
a game of crooked chance within a
spinning gyre.

viii
Will a hero soon arise? We listen
for a voice to prophesy. We wonder
what entrails must be removed to
make a hasty augury and what it
might foretell, as we wait, unable or
unwilling to break the terrible spell.

A Noble Experiment

Vultures on high
circle ever closer
in anticipation of
finding the corpse
still warm, splayed
out in a tawdry
landscape of needless
desolation.

What will be
the verdict of
the centuries?
How will they
explain the blind
suicidal urge,
the irrational rush
into the dark
singularity of
history?

Where Have All My Hopeful Words Gone?

Perhaps it is my own fault,
developing a sudden lack of artistry
when I need it the most

or, finally being unable to pry
away the choking grasp of depression,
I come up short.

Perhaps it is the words themselves,
as bruised and shell-shocked,
they seek refuge in the silence
of darkness,

unable to resist hiding their faces
and wondering in a mumbling way
when it might be safe to come back out
into the jack-booted light.

Burn

The eyes
of the zealots
burn with
an intense
flame.

It is not
the flame
of love.
It is not
the flame
of wisdom.
It is not
the flame
of liberty.

With their
blazing eyes,
the zealots
are saying:

we have cornered
the market on
what is right
and true.
If you are not
one of us,
we will be
coming for
you.

You cannot
hide from us.
We will find
you wherever
you are and we

will incinerate
your dreams.
We will
burn you
alive, with
our eyes.

Make Believe

Mommy and Daddy
have all the answers.
A kiss will make
it better.
Love makes the world
go round.
Everything works out
for the best.
All your sins will be
forgiven.
Heaven is waiting
for you on
the other side.

Don't be afraid
to speak your mind.
Truth and justice
will prevail.
Mobs won't hang
the innocent in
the public square.
Soldiers won't
gun down poets
on lonely back streets.
Nobody will come
for you in the middle
of the night and drag
you, screaming, into
the cold and desperate
air. Not here.

When the Bombs Come to Town

The bombs have finally
come to our small town
but not from the air.

They are on the ground
going door to door
asking if anyone is home.

No one is home
but the memories,
we say.

The bombs ignore us
and move on down
the streets pulling their
hair trigger personalities
and lethal aspirations behind
them in little red wagons.

The bombs are going door
to door and before they leave
they mark the front of each house
with a bloody X

and then walk on, pulling
their wagons behind them
and dreaming their bomb
dreams of rubble and char.

Dead Heroes

In the realm of the absurd
the absurd is commonplace.
And in this realm,
dead heroes have gathered
at a crossroads. It is
raining and their finely
tooled boots and fashionable
wingtips are getting muddy.

They look confused
because they do not know
how or why they are here.
Are they the unsuspecting
victims of a madman's
conjuration?
Are they somehow expected
to do something?

Arguments have broken
out and they are making
derisive comments about
one another. And they like
neither the rain nor the feel
of mud on their fine leather.

To the west are high and
jagged peaks, to the east a
dark river rages. To the south
is unchartered wilderness,
to the north the ruins of a
great city smolder and hiss
in the rain.

The dead heroes are resentful.
They do not even recognize
this country they are in.

They do not want to make
any more difficult choices.
They do not want to have
to petition the gods
once more for heroic luck.
They are content with the
comforting exaggerations
of history.

The dead heroes are obstinate
and do not move. They will
not choose north, south,
east or west. They will
choose nothing for this is not
their time to barter with fate
or flirt with firing squads in
a strange and wasted land.

They are glad to hear
a shrieking wind and see
the sky darkening with
large and ravenous crows.
They know the crows have
come from the other side
to gorge on the dead and
they look up at the sky
and smile as only dead
heroes can.

Asunder

i
All the masks are riddled
with bullets, all the eyes are
blurred with rage, love has
leaped from the steeple top
and the would-be heroes are
all in a daze.

ii
We have dared enshrine
the acts of fools to prove
a dark absurdity.
Trip wires abound in
the palace of despair.
Explosive devices are
everywhere we might
want to go except where
we don't need to be.
The human brain
has become a shapeless
lump of putty which
sculpts itself into
enigmatic pathways
for destructive terror.

We watch as the bones
of decency turn to ash,
as the ligaments of hope
explode and paint our
inner sky a gory red,
as people who should
know better morph into
canisters of hatred that
spit out a diminished
world.

iii
In the cathedral of existence
wolves cry and babies starve,
stars glimmer in mud puddles
and the sacred has no discernible
text, only a vague music which
inheres in the subatomic particles
of our imperfect understanding.
In the amorphous present,
the past and future blur into
one another. We wander here
somewhere near the edge of
meaning, hanging on to the
ragged rope ends of our lives,
unwilling to let go.

iv
I sift through my thoughts
as they hang upside down
like bats in an ancient barn.
Soon they will be on the wing,
hunting the night for tender
delicacies and yet will I even
know what to do with the
wriggling, captured prey?

v
Oh my love!
I want to reach for you
across the gaping divide
between thought and feeling,
carbon and silicon,
darkness and light,
so you may sooth me
with your innocence,
caress me with your hope,
but what have I for you
but kisses of dread, songs
of endless foreboding?

An American Girl

I just wanted to be beautiful
but they shot me in the face
I just wanted to sing
but they shot me in the throat
I just wanted to see
but they shot out my eyes
I just wanted to hear
but they shot off my ears
I just wanted to love
but they shot me through the heart
I just wanted to live
but they shot me,
they shot me dead.

Look as my blood flows
in the aisles of supermarkets
look as my blood flows
in churches and synagogues
look as my blood flows
in school classrooms
look as my blood flows
in movie theaters and dance halls
look as my blood flows
on the sidewalks
and down the streets
and into the storm drains
of America.

What Is This Beast Which As If From A Whirlwind Comes?

What is this beast which
as if from a whirlwind comes,
sucking the very sweetness
from the air?

What is this demon
that wraps itself
in a cloak of dread
and desolates the land
with foul fumes of rage?

What is this horror
that shatters hearts
with its evil voice
and sets the sky on fire
to mock the world?

Surely no human father
and no human mother could
have wrought such a fiend.

Surely it is not one of us.

Surely it has not come
because we have called for it.

Surely it has not come
because, in our ignorance
and fear,

we have begged it to come.

The Plains

A lightning strike

the great abandoned
cities are revealed
open to the night
festering sores
spread upon the earth
like a blight

a lightning strike

in the ghost land
the bison yet roam
with bones bleached white
the mystic herds
still sundered
by the old steel
now struggle to unite

a lightning strike

the weary myths
are dying
the taste of destiny
has soured
and the wind
rattles the dried
petals of prairie
flowers

a lightning strike

the plains are on fire
they burn and burn
far into the distances
of the combustible
night.

The Darkness of Light

It is not just the darkness
of night or the total lack of light
that can chill us so
but also the darkness that
dwells in light.

Search lights in towers,
a blinding flashlight in your face,
a bonfire light
where books are burned
or heretics set on fire,
the sun's first light
glimmering on the cold steel
of razor wire,

the mild light
of a pretty day
that just for a while
makes everything seem
all right
until you remember
we live also in
the darkness of light.

The Other Side of Silence

Behold, we know not anything;
I can but trust that good shall fall
At last -- far off-- at last, to all,
And every winter change to spring.

So runs my dream; but what am I?
An infant crying in the night;
An infant crying for the light;
And with no language but a cry

- Alfred, Lord Tennyson

i
All the months are getting cruel,
each in its own way,
distorting memory and desire,
breeding fire and ice,
droughts and plagues
and hard rains on unstable soil,
making us fend for ourselves,
making us arm up with insidious
intent like suspicious strangers in
a war-torn land.

We wait for news from the front
without knowing where the front is
or what it is or why
we are waiting for such news.

Perhaps the front is everywhere
in this hair trigger world:
in the corridors of power,
in the lost cities of despair,
in the palaces of greed,
out in the hinterlands
of the country's dying soul
where the old roads stub out
and rusting rails are being
sold for scrap and the last
days seem to be as near at hand
as Jesus billboards buckling
in an unforgiving sun.

ii
Far from the ivory towers
the God of Reason says
"rumors of my impending
death have not been exaggerated."
The God of Reason says
"I will not die from lynching
or stoning or from wild beasts
in the fields. I will die
from the slow suffocation
of irrelevance."
The God of Reason says
"the bone yards of history
accommodate many gods."

iii
And roaming still through
the ancient myths, Coyote
laughs his trickster laugh,
high and clear it echoes
through many canyons and
into the open spaces
where it is carried far and wide
by the indifferent wind.

O you who frolic
between the worlds,
engorged with life and
raffish cunning,
neither man nor beast
but part of all,
should we listen
to your midnight howls?

iv
Queen Isabella
what did you do?
The ghosts of this land
are looking for you.

So many bones
bleached white
in the sun,
Queen Isabella
what have you done?

v
Do you read the book
of bloody deeds
and hold it dear
for all to see
and shout it loudly
for all to hear
beneath the sun,
beyond the grave?

The masks we wear
in the mirrored house,
the disguises we seek
to make us real...
If the illusion stops,
our faces will fall
and land in heaps
behind the wall.

vi
I have a vision
obscenely repeating,
like a viral gif of doom,
of the unreal
cities of a lost
world where lies
cover the landscape
like volcanic dust,
like the lethal slime
of radioactive waste,
like the charnel vomit
of a deranged god.

I see the addicts
of mendacity
with sunken eyes
and hollow limbs
haunting the streets
beneath flickering lights
extending boney arms
to the few who pass
in a conspiracy
of resentment like
lepers of old let loose
from the dens of time.

And I see
myself among them,
slack jawed, unable
to comprehend,
looking for something
I cannot define.

vii
Let us go then
you and I,
but where?
Where is the bruised
heart of America?
Dean Moriarity is dead
and we have lost our way.
The road to Montgomery
is closed for repairs.
We took a wrong turn
off the interstate
and road kill zombies
are seeking our blood.

viii
Death enters the room
and draws up a chair.
Voltaire is dealt
the dead man's hand
and stout Cortes
wears a belt of skulls
as holy scribes write
what the world must read.

The unreal will come
to devour the real,
a ravenous monster
no one can stop.
The beast, the beast
will come at last
to gorge upon
its mother's flesh.

ix
What dreams are these
which break like glass
upon a beach of
hardened stone?

Dreams of dominion
dreams of gold
dreams of sinew and blood
dreams of cloven chains
and open arms
dreams of polished metal
and circuit boards of doom
dreams which hurtle
through the maw of time
dreams of dreams
bringing tears from
the naked land.

x
Does the sea remember
the names of its dead?
Does the earth give up
its bones to the wind?

As mermaids cry out
on the shrinking strand,
a girl from Treblinka
rides the waves.
Her face dissolves
before she falls
without a word
beneath the swells.

xi
Running out
of time and metaphors,
a swordless hero with
rickety knees moves
across a question mark
with its point erased
and its curvy remnant
stretched taut
like a high wire
over an abyss
with no safety net,
and there is no turning
around and no
going back,
no matter what may
lie on the other side.

xii
Double helix, yin and yang,
leptons and quarks,
the love songs we sang
to Callicles and Pan,
the futile quest we've made
for the brotherhood of man.

Over the pathways
of the centuries
the Zeitgeist moves
in mysterious ways.
Hegelian rhapsody
Orwellian fugue,
Heisenberg shuffle,
mushroom clouds
obscure the view.

While trap and mumble rap
steal the night's applause,
the shadow world takes
what it cannot give
and gamers play as if
for keeps within the walls
of Wonderland.

xiii
All has changed
and nothing has changed.

O Ozymandias,
King of Kings
with sneer of
cold command,
where can we find
your mighty works?

The anointed one
grins his TV grin
as the cameras roll
again and again
with dark faced
pawns to hide a sin.
Fair is foul
and foul is fair.
Up is down and
down is up,
as deep we breathe
the electric air.

The restless human
herd is spooked
and on the move.
The eyes are wild
and full of ire.
The booted feet are
ready to begin a
desperate stampede.

And will evil's craven
banality soon appear,
in thought and word
and deed?

xiv

In the name of the father
permission is granted

in the name of the son
permission is granted

in the name of all the ghosts
who wander still in restless haunts
permission is granted

to lie
to cheat
to steal
to hate
to plunder
to rape
to defame
to kill

in the name
of all that is holy
and all that is good
permission is granted

by those who
always have
and always will.

XV
The blur of life,
the muddled path,
at the cusp of
future and past
our liminal lives
like shadows surreal
play out upon a
distorted screen.

Where is truth
and where the lie?
We choose our sides
on shifting sands
and circle our rage
to make our stand.

xvi
What is the half-life of hope?
What are the contingencies of grace?
What is redemption's price?

O where are the dark eyed
daughters I have never known?

Holding hands beneath
a stand of cottonwoods
and crafting songs for
the muted sky.

xvii
Razor wire and the ghost
of Jacob Schmid,
white rose petals fall
and then they bleed.
Put the headless ones
in unmarked graves
and have a cup
of sweetened tea.

The lecterns are empty
the pulpits are full
the pews are crowded
the libraries closed,
so many undone
by hate's moreish taste,
so many uncounted
by the nightly news.

Yank the innocents
from the streets.
Close the borders
and build a wall.
Count your blessings
as the petals fall.

xviii
Hate is love
and lies are truth.

Ring around the rosie
Pocket full of posies

Hate the truth
and love the lies.

Ashes to ashes,
We all fall down.

O my country,
'tis for thee I cry.

xix
Hello silence
my long lost friend,
I've come to visit
once again.

The world's chatter
has a deadly feel and
the post-modern logos
has taken a spin
at light speed out
on a phantom road
and can't find its
way back again
from the mazy streets
of Crazy Town.

Hello silence
my long lost friend,
refugees from
the strident din,
weary and worn,
are lining up
outside your
chamber door.

Please let us in.

xx
The river is wide and
the levees are burning
the bridges are falling
the boats are leaking
the water is full
of baptized bodies
drowning, drowning,
and the winged air
is wild with vicious
beaks and shrieking
cries.

Who now will lead
the danse macabre
and who will march
to the steady beat
in a coffle file
along the river bank
a thousand miles
to where the shining
sea in mourning lies?

xxi
Wind whistles
through skull eyes
on the southern plains,
the tracks are gone,
no more trains,
and the lines are long
for the east-bound stage.

Slavers and ravers
jostle and shove,
hustlers and rustlers
load their guns,
the ladies of the night
left a week ago
and the last drink
was drunk
by a desperado,
now slowly swinging
above the bar.

Beneath the sun
Quanah Parker waits.
The clouds of dust
will be easy to see
and the taste of blood
will be as sweet
as only the taste of
blood can be.

xxii
Take from
the forge of justice
a hammered wrath
and send it forth
as a sword of light.

Make the darkness
fall back, make it
shrink in fear,
make it devour itself
in utter despair.

Such power unleashed
could cleave the world
or else make whole and
new the fissured land.

Yet who can wield
a weapon of such
wondrous woe
with discerning eye
and steady hand?

xxiii
The days are drawn
and quartered,
the nights are burned
at the stake,
my eyes
are quarantined,
my throat is the throat
of a wounded bystander
clogged with ashes,
gasping for air,
trying to speak
something of consequence,
something vital,
something that matters,
from the other side
of silence.

Notes

The title has been taken from a line by Lawrence Ferlinghetti in *A Coney Island of the Mind.*

i

Purposefully reminiscent of T.S. Eliott's beginning lines of *The Wasteland*

iii

Coyote. as Trickster appears in a number of mythic traditions but often with the same magical powers of transformation, resurrection, and medicine. He sometimes is portrayed as fighting against monsters with help from the Spirit Chief. The trickster archetype in all myths is known as a catalyst for change.

vii

Dean Moriarity (i.e. Neal Cassady) is a reference to the main character in Jack Kerouac's *On the Road.*

xii

Callicles was a character in Plato's *Gorgias* who argues that might makes right and the end justifies the means.

xvii

Jacob Schmid was a janitor at Ludwig Maximilian University in Munich, Germany. In February 1943 he turned in Hans Scholl and Sophie Scholl, siblings who were members of the Nazi resistance group White Rose, for handing out pamphlets. They were turned over to the Gestapo, tried for treason, and guillotined.

xxi

Quanah Parker was a war leader of the famously bellicose Comanche nation. He was the son of a Comanche chief and a white woman. Quanah Parker later made peace, embraced much of White culture, and became a wealthy rancher.

About the Author

Kendall Bradley is a native of Accomack County on the Eastern Shore of Virginia and is a graduate of the University of Virginia. He is the author of five other books of verse: *Backwater Moon*, *A Butterfly with Teeth*, *Vicinity of Time*, *At the Edge of Mercy*, and *Backwater Musings*. He lives in the small town of Melfa with his lovely wife, muse, and best friend, Ronda.

www.ingramcontent.com/pod-product-compliance
Lightning Source LLC
Chambersburg PA
CBHW041927090426
42743CB00021B/3469